Storytelling Through Art

By Riker Matters

Illustrated by Cassandra Bynder

We respect and honour Aboriginal and Torres Strait Islander Elders past, present and future. We acknowledge the stories, traditions and living cultures of Aboriginal and Torres Strait Islander peoples on this land and commit to building a brighter future together.

Library For All Ltd.

Riker Matters, author

Cassandra Bynder, illustrator

My name is Riker Matters. I have used art as a way to share knowledge, tell my story, and communicate all my life.

This cultural practice is second nature to me, as it is something my family has always done.

In a Noongar family full of artists, this part of our culture has remained strong.

In this book, I have gathered some examples of how different Aboriginal peoples in Australia have used and continue to use storytelling through art.

In Australia, there are many different Aboriginal language and skin groups. Shared among these groups is a love of storytelling.

In the past, Aboriginal Australians did not have a written language, but they shared knowledge and stories through conversation and visual language, like art.

Just like our people, there is great diversity in our art styles. Some groups use symbols, dot paintings or rock art. Some groups use body painting, ceremony or wood carvings.

These art forms are all types of storytelling.

From our stories of creation to our modern storytelling, we are proud to preserve and pass on our knowledge and culture through art.

The meanings of symbols and art styles are different from state to state, and Country to Country. But there are similarities too.

Let's explore some of the different ways Aboriginal Australians practise storytelling through art.

The Noongar (Bibbulmun) people of Western Australia passed down knowledge verbally, using oral storytelling as one of their art forms.

This is still practised today by the Bibbulmun people, within their families, between their Elders, and among groups.

In the past, the Mowanjum Kimberley people in northern Western Australia practised ochre painting and rock art. They used this art to depict Dreaming stories, mark special and sacred places, and share knowledge.

They created sacred ceremonial places where depictions of Wandjinas (spirit people) can still be seen and cherished today.

The people of Arnhem Land in the Northern Territory are one group who traditionally used x-ray art. This is the practice of depicting animals or humans using skeletal frames and internal organs as features.

This style of art shows connection and understanding of Country and its inhabitants. People who used this art style had a deep understanding of the natural world, with a scientific knowledge of the inner workings of flora and fauna. They understood the land on which they lived and survived.

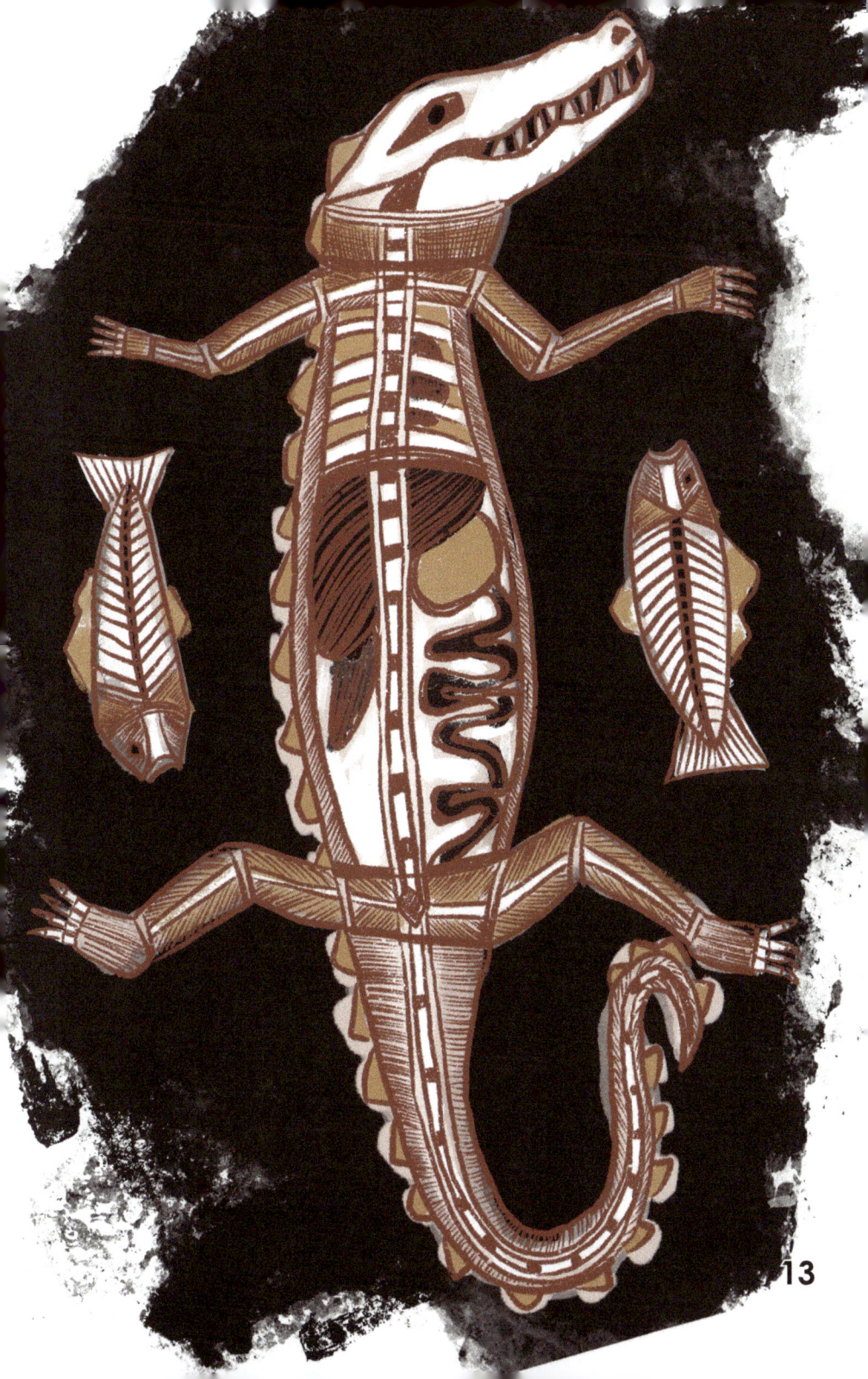

The Central Western Desert people were among the first to use dot paintings, a type of art that is very popular across Australia and commonly associated with Aboriginal culture. Every dot in these paintings has meaning. The colours, positions and clusters are symbolic and tell stories about people and Country.

Nowadays, many groups practise this style for fun, business, teaching, and to bring people together. But the importance of each individual dot is still recognised by artists who use this medium.

Another art style used by many groups is symbology.

Artists use symbols to depict native wildlife, Country, foods and people. It is an abstract way of representing parts of life and telling stories about Dreaming and recent events.

Symbology means creators can express complex ideas and opinions while showing joy and beauty through creative art.

Other ways Aboriginal people tell stories is through sculptures or carvings in wood. These objects can be created specifically for artistic purposes, or used for various daily needs, while still being used as a canvas for storytelling.

For example, tools, weapons and ceremonial instruments can be seen with stories carved or burned onto them.

Today, popular objects like the didgeridoo, boomerang and animal sculptures are made by combining the knowledge passed down by our Elders with the perspecitives of modern artists.

Body painting in traditional practices and ceremony is used by many tribes as a way of sharing knowledge. Sometimes people are painted to look like animals. Other times, they are painted to make a connection with the land.

Some ceremonial dances done by people in body paint are shared with everyone, while others are special and can only be performed within tribal groups.

All of these art forms are practised today by contemporary Aboriginal artists and storytellers.

We teach it in schools and at lecture halls. We tell stories to each other, share with our kin and with others who ask.

The art created by Aboriginal people keeps our culture alive. It continues the practice of sharing knowledge about local areas, about the past, the present, and the future.

Storytelling and art reach back through our past and settle with us in the present. In this way, we continue to tell our stories and learn from our Elders.

These are some of the traditional tools that were used and are still used today.

Traditional	Modern
Ochre: artists still use ochre in their work. Sometimes this is true ochre, or it might be acrylic paint in ochre colours.	Acrylic paints: popular among many traditional and contemporary artists.
Sticks: a good way to make detailed markings and dot work.	Paint brushes: most artists use paint brushes today as their main tool of choice. The bottom of the brush handle is used for dot painting, too.
Paperbark: taken from the paperbark tree and dried out to make a good canvas for art.	Canvas: fabric canvases are a top choice for artists today, as they are easy to access and long lasting.
Sharp rocks: perfect for adding detailed markings and carvings.	Carving tools: a more controlled and reliable choice for making markings.

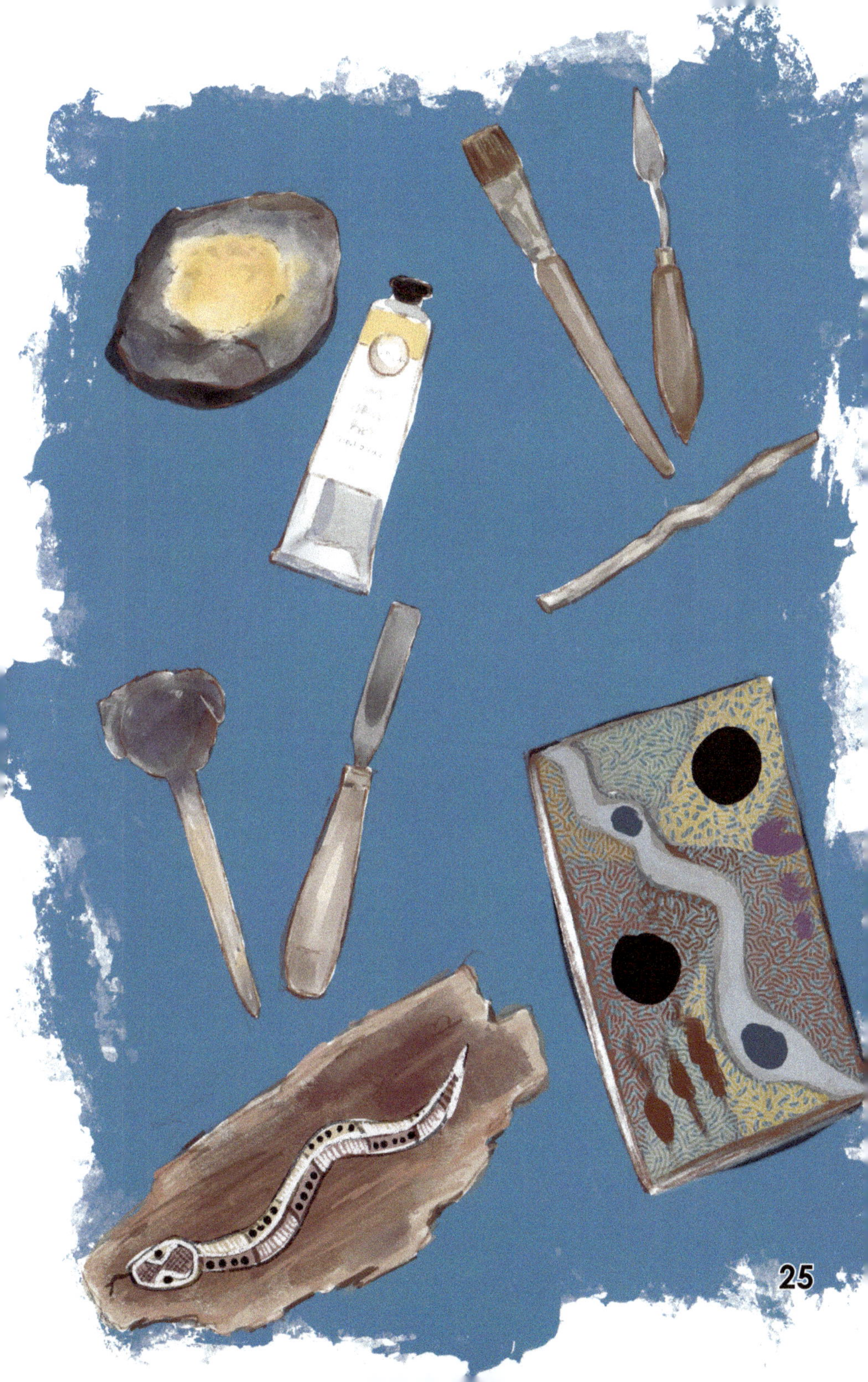

Glossary

Term	Definition
Culture	The language, customs, ideas, and art of a group of people.
Ceremony	A formal act or series of acts done in a particular way for a special occasion.
Wandjinas	Cloud and rain spirits from Australian Aboriginal mythology.
X-Ray art	An art form where animals and humans are depicted by drawing or painting the skeletal frame and internal organs.
Symbology	An object or image that represents something else.
Traditional practices	The handing-down of a culture's beliefs and customs from parents to children over many years.
Contemporary	Modern or current time.
Kin	Family.

You can use these questions to talk about this book with your family, friends and teachers.

What did you learn from this book?

Describe this book in one word. Funny? Scary? Colourful? Interesting?

How did this book make you feel when you finished reading it?

What was your favourite part of this book?

About the contributors

Riker is a Noongar artist from Perth, Western Australia, with extensive experience in acrylic painting, digital art, illustration and design. Inspiration comes to Riker in all forms; she draws from the Earth, the Ocean, and what connects her emotionally to Country and soul.

Cassandra Bynder is a Ballardong-Whadjuk Noongar woman raised in the south west of Western Australia on Wadandi Noongar Country. She loves taking long coastal hikes with her kids and teaching art skills to the community. One of her favourite books when she was little was the *Faraway Tree* series by Enid Blyton.

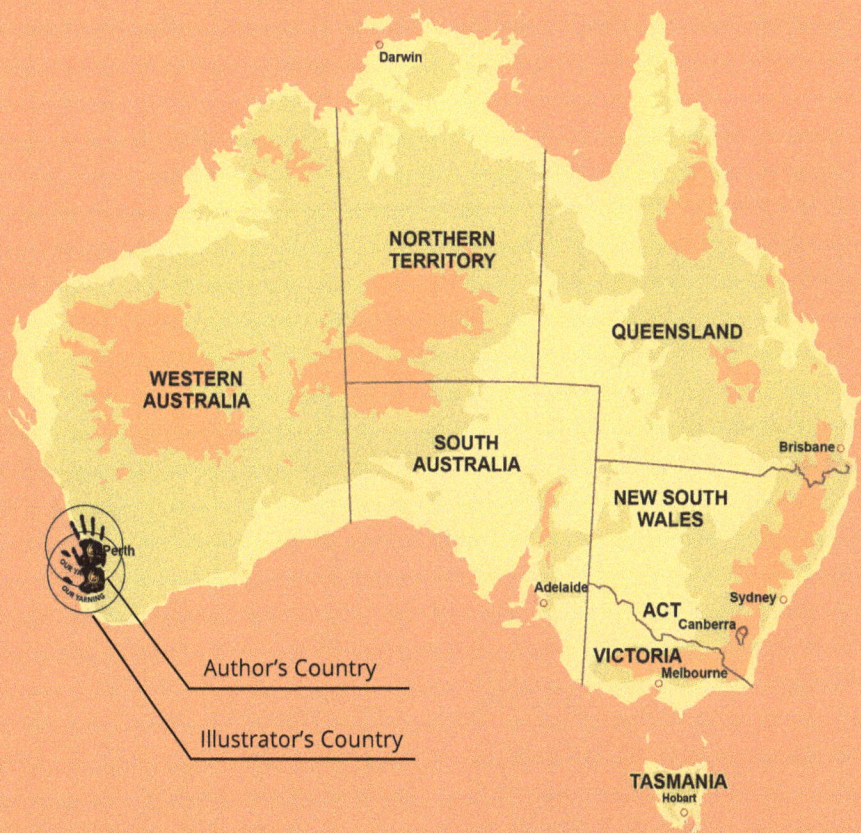

Darwin

NORTHERN
TERRITORY

QUEENSLAND

WESTERN
AUSTRALIA

SOUTH
AUSTRALIA

Brisbane

NEW SOUTH
WALES

Perth

Adelaide

Sydney

ACT
Canberra

VICTORIA

Melbourne

Author's Country

Illustrator's Country

TASMANIA
Hobart

Our Yarning

The Our Yarning collection aligns with the Australian Curriculum through the Cross-Curriculum Priorities — Aboriginal and Torres Strait Islander Histories and Cultures. The collection provides an authentic opportunity for learning and embedding Aboriginal and Torres Strait Islander perspectives because it is written by Aboriginal and Torres Strait Islander people.

We know that children learn better, and enjoy reading more, when they see themselves in the stories, characters and illustrations of the books they read.

To download the app, visit the Google Play Store or Apple Store and search 'Our Yarning'.

libraryforall.org

You're reading Upper Primary

Learner – Beginner readers

Start your reading journey with short words,
big ideas and plenty of pictures.

Level 1 – Rising readers

Raise your reading level with more words,
simple sentences and exciting images.

Level 2 – Eager readers

Enjoy your reading time with familiar words,
but complex sentences.

Level 3 – Progressing readers

Develop your reading skills with creative stories
and some challenging vocabulary.

Level 4 – Fluent readers

Step up your reading skills with playful narratives,
new words and fun facts.

Middle Primary – Curious readers

Discover your world through science and stories.

Upper Primary – Adventurous readers

Explore your world through science and stories.

Storytelling Through Art

First published 2024

Published by Library For All Ltd
Email: info@libraryforall.org
URL: libraryforall.org

Our Yarning logo design by Jason Lee, Bidjipidji Art

Original illustrations by Cassandra Bynder

Storytelling Through Art
Matters, Riker
ISBN: 978-1-923376-31-1
SKU04428